Everything You Need To Know About

STREET GANGS

Evidence of street gangs can be seen in cities all over North
America.

Everything You Need To Know About

STREET GANGS

Evan Stark, Ph.D., M.S.W.

THE ROSEN PUBLISHING GROUP, INC.
NEW YORK

Published in 1992, 1995 by The Rosen Publishing Group, Inc.
29 East 21st Street, New York,, New York 10010

Revised Edition 1995
Copyright © 1992, 1995 by The Rosen Publishing Group, Inc.

Printed in the United States of America.

Library of Congress Cataloging-in-Publication Data

Stark, Evan
    Everything you need to know about street gangs / Evan Stark.
    (The Need to know library)
    Includes bibliographical references and index.
    Summary: Examines the phenomenon of street gangs, the reasons people join
them, the danger they can hold, and ways of avoiding getting involved with them
    ISBN 0-8239-2121-2
    1. Gangs—United States—Juvenile literature. [1. Gangs.]
I. Title. II. Series.
HV6439.U5S73   1991
364.1'06'60973—dc20   91-4779
                                    CIP
                                      AC

Contents

Introduction   6

1. Johnny's Story   9

2. Information about Gangs   13

3. Johnny's Questions—and Some Answers   21

4. Are Gangs New?   29

5. Why Do Young People Join Gangs?   35

6. Breaking the Law   41

7. Girls, Gangs, and Sex Roles   47

8. The Guardian Angels   51

9. Another Way of Fighting   55

Glossary–Explaining New Words   60

Where to Get Help   61

For Further Reading   62

Index   63

Introduction

Wherever there are young people, there are gangs. Gangs have existed since time began.

Today it is estimated that there are as many as 52,000 youth gang members in the United States, including 5,000 girls. Most come from the poorest inner cities. But there are also gangs in wealthier areas, in big cities and in small Midwestern towns.

A total of 2,829 people under 18 were arrested for murder and manslaughter in 1992, 40 percent of whom were white. That same year, 63,683 young people were arrested for aggravated assault, 56 percent of whom were white. Gangs are a part of life.

In 1993, three gang members were convicted of killing a 17-year-old girl for her car keys. These gang members were not in Los Angeles or New York. They were from Davenport, Iowa, a city with fewer than 100,000 residents.

Joining a gang may seem like a good idea. It may seem exciting, or a good way to make friends for life. However, the decision to join a gang can be a decision to ruin your life. Thousands of teenagers in gangs are killed every year; many more are left paralyzed for life from gunshot wounds.

When you join a gang, you give your future away. Employers who will hire gang members are few and far between. A program was begun in San Jose, California, to remove gang tattoos for members who wanted to begin a normal life. Since most members get tattoos of gang insignia at some point in their life, the program had a lot of success. Even if you are able to quit a gang, you are in danger of rival gangs because of the tattoos you might still bear.

You pay a big price when you join a gang. You give up your freedom and any choices you might have in your life. The gang tells you what to do and where and when to do it. To stay in a gang, you often have to break the law. In some gangs, this may mean killing another person.

The most dangerous gangs are created to make money by selling drugs. These are often called *posses*. Members of posses care about nothing but making money. They always carry guns.

Twenty years ago, the leading concerns in school were cutting class and the way students dressed. Today, you may have to walk through a metal detector before going into class. You might be scared to go to school because of gang violence.

You probably have many questions about gangs. You might even be considering joining a gang. This book will answer your questions and tell you what gang life is really like.

The Hell's Angels are one of the largest and most powerful gangs
in the world.

Chapter 1

Johnny's Story

Johnny Boston moved with his mother to a city in New England when he was 13. He had lived his entire life in Cleveland, and had never been in the Northeast before. His father had died when he was seven, and his mother worked as a nurse.

Johnny was big for his age, both tall and strong. He did well in school, especially in math. He had been very happy at his old school.

He wondered whether he would get along at his new school. He was a little worried that he wouldn't make any friends there. The school was five blocks away from his house on Kensington Street. As he walked to school on his first day, he noticed a group of boys on the corner. They were wearing baggy jeans and green suede jackets with the letters KSI on the back. Two of the boys had pagers on their belts, and several had brand-new expensive basketball sneakers.

Johnny was impressed. That night he asked his mother for a pair of nice sneakers, and she said they couldn't afford them. "We need furniture for the new apartment," she told him. "So for now you'll have to make do with what you have." Johnny understood, but he still wished he could get a pair.

School went well for Johnny. He really liked his math teacher, Mrs. Parley. Whenever he solved a particularly hard problem in class, she would say, "Well done, Mr. Boston." That embarrassed Johnny, but it also made him feel proud. And he liked being called "Mr." It made him feel important. Soon he noticed one of the girls in class looking at him.

Then one day, when Johnny was leaving school, he saw a group of girls giggling. The girl who had looked at him in class was one of them. They were pointing at him. He was sure it was because of his clothes. Johnny felt very small.

That night Johnny and his mother had an argument. Johnny wanted to tell her about the girls, but talking about that with his mother made him uncomfortable. So he sulked instead. When his mom asked what was wrong, he bit her head off.

At school, everyone knew about KSI. It was a drug posse. The letters stood for Kensington Street International. Most of the members cut school, and they always seemed to have money.

A few days later Johnny was hanging out with some new friends. A man in a new white car was watching him. He called Johnny over to the car and

asked him to get in. Then he asked Johnny if he
needed money.

"Always," Johnny replied, trying to sound cool.

"You're strong, you're smart. Do you want to be
down with the brothers?" the man asked. Johnny
then guessed that the man was a drug dealer and
was asking him to join KSI.

"Your job is easy," the man continued. "You start
as a lookout. You get a walkie-talkie. If you see any
trouble, you let me know. You wear the colors. And
you get $60 a day to start. Do well, you'll get more."

"How much more?" Johnny asked, not believing
he actually asked the question.

The man laughed. "Enough."

"What about school?" Johnny asked. The man
stared at him until Johnny felt like an idiot.

"Hey, you go to school so you can get a job, right?
Well, this is the best job you'll ever have. Think it
over." The man gave Johnny $10.

Next the man took Johnny to meet the other KSI
brothers. They all shook his hand, and he felt really
important. "Do you have a piece?" one of them asked.
Johnny shook his head. He'd never even seen a
handgun except on TV.

That night Johnny lay awake, wondering what to
do. What would his father have done? That was no
help—his father was dead. He really needed money.
He wanted new sneakers, new clothes. He was sick
of feeling like people were laughing at him at school.

People said KSI was dangerous. But to him they

seemed friendly enough. Anyway, if there was trouble he could handle himself. He could always quit the gang if things got really rough.

The talk about a "piece" scared him, though. And he liked school and didn't want to leave. But he liked the idea of having a walkie-talkie and being part of a group like KSI, too. He wanted his mother to be proud of him. She'd be happy if he told her he had a job and gave her a little money every week.

He thought people who used drugs were stupid. But the dealer seemed cool. You didn't have to be a user to be a dealer. Johnny added figures in his head. If he joined the gang, after a while he could even buy a computer.

Johnny stayed awake all night trying to decide what to do. Should he work as a lookout for KSI? Should he lie to his mother? Is working in a drug gang really the best job he could ever get? Should he get a gun? How should he decide about the gang? Who could advise him?

Chapter 2

Information about Gangs

Thousands of young people face the same tough decision as Johnny Boston every year: Should I join a gang? The more informed you are, the better you can cope with the problem.

Gang Organization

As mentioned before, it is estimated that there are as many as 52,000 youth gang members in the United States alone. Gang members usually, but not always, come from the poorest inner-city areas.

Gangs often form along racial or ethnic lines. They have all kinds of reasons for forming, from cultural solidarity to drug trafficking. The one thing that all gangs have in common is a claim on a turf, or territory. A gang's turf may be one block, a neighborhood, or an entire area of the city. Members wear the gang's colors, or specific style of clothing. Each gang has a leader, and sometimes other officers.

Gangs exist by the hundreds and are found in almost 200 cities in the US. Some are small and informal, hanging out on only one street. Others, like KSI, are much better organized. Although they make their home on only one street, they may recruit members and smaller groups from all over the city.

Drug gangs are different from other kinds of gangs. They are much more organized, and much more dangerous. They are responsible for the distribution of illegal drugs, from marijuana to cocaine. This involves selling the drugs, carrying large amounts of cash, and protecting the dealer from police or rival gangs.

Drug posses are almost always controlled by an adult whom most gang members never meet. They are formed solely for the purpose of making money. Risks are taken, not for adventure, but for profit. They are the most dangerous type of gang.

Some gangs have several thousand members and chapters in cities around the United States. The most famous alliances are the Crips and the Bloods, two rival gangs that began in Los Angeles. Some gangs even have branches in prison.

Gang Life

A gang is any group with a name and a turf to defend. It may mark its turf with graffiti on the streets or the walls of buildings.

Many gangs have emblems or special jackets. Some wear bandannas, or "rags," of a specific color around the head or hung loosely out of the back pocket. They usually have some form of colors.

Many street gangs are involved in illegal activities, most often selling drugs.

Leaders may be called "jefes," "honchos," "chiefs," or "generals." A branch of a large gang has an over-all gang leader, called the "kingpin."

One of the attractive things about gangs is the loyalty the members all have for each other. They seem to value the other members of their gang more than themselves. Gangs seem to provide an instant group of best friends.

The bad side of this loyalty is that you can never have friends outside the gang. You spend all your time with the gang. You must do whatever the gang leader tells you to do. You lose your freedom when you join a gang.

Contrary to popular belief, life in a gang can be very boring. Most of the time, members sit around waiting for something to happen. When something finally does, it is very brief, and then the members return to the waiting.

In order to join a gang, you have to prove you are worthy by going through a process of *initiation*. In some gangs, initiation involves committing some kind of crime. In others, new members have to "walk the line," that is, walk along a line of members while each member beats him. Sometimes the recruit is told that for the next week he will be attacked by gang members without warning, and he is ordered not to fight back. Initiations are generally very brutal.

Brian Watkins was visiting New York City from Salt Lake City, Utah during the summer of 1992. He

Members of gangs often prefer to socialize only with other members of their gang.

A lookout working for a gang keeps watch for approaching police
or rival gang members during drug deals and other business.

was attacked on the subway and killed. His murderer was soon arrested and explained to the police that he had to mug a tourist to get into the Dukes, a local gang. This was their initiation. Now the young recruit will probably spend the rest of his life in jail.

Gang Violence

Today the use of guns is quite common in gangs. Shootings committed by gang members are on the rise. In 1991 there were more than 350 gang-related killings in Los Angeles alone. Many of these involved *drive-by* shootings, when gang members fire guns out the windows of a speeding car at their enemies.

Most gang shootings involve other gang members. But recently more and more innocent bystanders have been killed by gang shootings. In 1988 the number of bystanders killed in gang violence rose 90 percent. The same year, the number of gang members killed by members of their own gang also rose 90 percent, as members become more and more careless of whom they shoot. Members are also usually bad shots.

A gang's main duty is usually to protect its turf. Simply wearing another gang's colors on a gang's turf is reason enough to be killed. The killing of a gang member usually provokes a revenge killing, which in turn provokes a revenge killing, and on and on. Sometimes gangs go *wilding*, that is, go on a rampage, breaking windows, looting, attacking bystanders, committing rape, even murder.

A smaller gang may form alliances with other groups from the same neighborhood. They may then attack the groups in another neighborhood in a gang war. Many innocent people, as well as the gang members themselves, may be hurt or killed in a gang war.

Someone who joins a gang usually completes his life in one of two ways: jail or death. Gangs can make you feel important, can make you feel that you belong, can make you feel rich. But they are not worth the destruction they cause, both in the members' lives and in the community.

Chapter 3

Johnny's Questions— and Some Answers

Johnny Boston had to decide whether to join KSI. He had a number of questions about gangs. Answering these questions might help you think of advice for someone like Johnny.

Can I Join a Gang and Still Keep My Best Friends Outside the Gang?

When you join a gang, your first and only loyalty is to the gang. This makes it hard to keep your other friends.

Kemal Davis and Mark Star had been friends since first grade. They lived in different neighborhoods but played basketball on the same team. When Kemal joined a gang called the Panthers, Mark told him he was making a mistake. "You're not anybody unless you're in a gang," Kemal replied.

One day, a member of the Panthers dissed Mark in school. When Mark walked away, the boy pushed him. Mark was not afraid, but he didn't want trouble. And he knew the boy belonged to a gang. Suddenly the boy from the gang pulled a knife. "I'll be waiting for you after school," he told Mark.

Mark was scared. He didn't want to tell anyone at school—that would be "finking." But he also didn't want to get stabbed. Mark decided to protect himself. He told the principal, and the gang member was removed from school.

Soon after, the Panthers ordered Kemal to trick Mark into coming to the playground. They reminded Kemal of the gang rule: When one member is harmed, everyone seeks revenge. Kemal didn't want Mark hurt. But he was afraid for his own safety. So he went along with the plan. When Mark got to the playground, the Panthers knocked him down. They cut him so badly he lost an eye. To this day, Kemal cannot forget the look on Mark's face when he realized what Kemal, his friend, had done.

Young people are often fiercely loyal. At the same time, they worry about whether others will be loyal to them. The loyalty of a gang is an important attraction. If you are in a gang, when someone in the gang is hurt, you take revenge. It doesn't even matter who was right or wrong. But gang loyalty has a price. It means you can't decide for yourself what is right or wrong. You can't disagree with the gang. As a result, loyalty to a gang usually means giving up your friends outside the gang.

Some teens join gangs to end feelings of loneliness and isolation.

Most gangs resort to violence for a number of reasons. Often, they are defending their turf or seeking revenge for an action that has been taken against one of their members.

Why Can't I Just Quit?

Many kids think they can join a gang and then leave when trouble starts or when they want to move on with their lives. But when you leave a gang, its members treat you like an enemy. Some gangs only make you walk the line again, and once you have done so you are no longer a member. However, in most gangs leaving is not so simple. You may be watched because the gang members think you will tell people their secrets. You may be killed for being a risk. It's especially dangerous to leave a posse. These gangs have more to lose than other gangs, and less gang loyalty.

Do I Have to Break the Law in a Gang?

Some of the things gangs do are harmless. Their actions may be aimed more at rebelling against parents than at harming others. However, almost every gang breaks some law routinely. It may be as minor as vandalism, doing things like spray-painting the gang's symbol on buildings, to theft, to murder.

Some gangs are primarily social. They hang out together, support one another in school, play sports on the street. Once in a while, however, they may steal a car, smoke marijuana or drink alcohol, or get into a fight.

Some gangs' activities center around finding other gangs and getting into fights, sometimes called *rumbling*. They attack people for fun or profit. Drug posses like KSI focus all their activity around making money from selling drugs. They carry guns and have no qualms about using them.

Will I Have to Carry a Gun?

Everyone in KSI carried a gun because of the business they did. One gang member, having left his gang, said to a reporter: "It's better for the police to catch you with a gun than for your enemies to catch you without one. They cut you into pieces in a bathtub. They dump you in dumpsters all over town. To us, guns are more important than women. Guns are what keep you alive. I never go to sleep without my gun. I can't trust anybody."

Being in a gang means having a piece of iron as your best friend. You can't even really trust the other members of your gang. You carry a gun, and it is the only thing you love.

Will I Get Rich?

Some people think gang members are rich, drive expensive cars, and don't have to work. However, even in a drug posse, very few people get rich. Most of their money goes in one hand and out the other to support flash and style rather than for living. They do not live luxurious or glamorous lives.

Drug dealing is actually hard and dangerous work. It begins early in the morning and lasts until late in the night. You work seven days a week. There are no vacations, no sick days. You are always on the job. You probably have a pager so that people who want to buy can get in touch with you whenever they feel like it. Your time is not your own.

The work is incredibly dangerous. You must always be on guard, watching for police or rival gangs. You are constantly in danger of being killed. The odds of surviving are not high in your favor.

You don't even own your own car. You share it with many other drug dealers. It belongs to the kingpin.

Sometimes drug dealers do make more money than they would otherwise. But they give up their freedom and often their lives for it. Is it worth it?

Native Americans have traditionally been members of tribes, which are groups of people who share similar dress and codes of behavior. Tribes are not gangs.

Chapter 4

Are Gangs New?

Ever since people could walk, they have been organizing themselves into distinct groups.

Group rituals were part of how Native American boys became men. The same is true of many other tribes throughout the world. From Africa to Australia, from Japan to Canada, certain rituals have united people together in a group. Gangs also demonstrate group behavior. In Europe when someone did something wrong, a gang of children would paint their faces, go to that person's house, and bang on pots and pans. When the wrongdoer came out, they would force him or her to march through the town. This was called *rough music*.

Gangs often have a special way of dressing. One way of dressing adopted by these historical gangs was called the *peaky blinder*. Boys who wore a peaky blinder shaved their heads and wore long, peaked caps, a row of brass buttons on their coats, wide leather belts, and pants that were wide at the bottom. They resembled the groups we call "punks" or "skinheads" today.

In the United States, there were all sorts of gangs. Around the time of the Civil War, children left their families and went to work while they were still very young. They formed gangs that hung around saloons.

Because there was so much sickness, many children lost their parents and became homeless. Without real families, these children banded together and formed gangs. Boys and girls as young as nine years old would join a gang headed by an older boy. The gang would live in a small apartment or basement. The gang members made money any way they could. Often they would beg, steal, or sell newspapers or flowers from a small wagon. At the end of each day, they would give some of the money to the older boy.

There were also large gangs of young men. Before cities had fire departments, a giant bell would ring when there was a fire. Gangs from all over the city would race to see who could get to the fire first and put it out. These gangs wore fancy clothes and had names like Dead Rabbits or Bowery Boys. Other gangs were known as Shirt Tails, Bloods, Roach Guards, and Old Maid's Boys.

Sometimes, when times were hard and there was no work or money in the city, gangs would join

Motorcycle gangs often look scary, but many of them are relatively harmless.

together and riot. When this happened, buildings were often set on fire. Since many of the buildings were made of wood, fires spread rapidly and caused much more damage than they would today. Riots led by city gangs could involve thousands of people. Sometimes the army was needed to stop riots led by gangs.

Much later, in the 1920s, criminal gangs developed in the United States. In those days, it was illegal to buy and sell liquor. This was called *Prohibition*. Criminal gangs made their own liquor and sold it to people who wanted to drink. These gangs were called mobs. Mobs fought gang wars to control the money made by selling illegal liquor. One famous mob leader was Al Capone, who was known as "Scarface."

Most gangs develop their own style of dress and their own secret
code for communication between members.

In the 1950s there was a famous musical play about gangs called *West Side Story.* In the play there are two gangs, the Jets and the Sharks. The Jets are an Anglo gang and the Sharks are Puerto Rican. Tony, a young man from the Jets, falls in love with Maria, whose brother is a Shark. When Tony tries to stop a fight between the rival gangs, there is a rumble and he is killed.

The gangs of the 1950s, like those in *West Side Story*, were mostly involved in small-time crime. Most of their violence was directed toward other gangs at rumbles. Few if any guns or knives were used. Like the Jets and Sharks in the play, these gangs hung around candy stores. They spent most of their time talking, playing sports, going to the movies, looking for girls, or driving around. Sometimes they had a clubhouse where they held dances, smoked marijuana, or drank beer. Those who wore their hair long and matted down with grease were called "greasers." They wore fancy colored satin jackets with their names printed on the back.

In the fifties, gang fights often centered on having *heart*. To show that he had heart, a boy would have to prove himself by fighting another boy. This action was much like the rituals of Native American children many years before. People were often hurt in rumbles, but few people were killed.

There are still many youth gangs like the ones pictured in *West Side Story.* One difference is that today, the gangs include Vietnamese Americans, Chinese Americans, and Mexican Americans, as well as other ethnic groups. Another important difference is that today's gang member is much more likely to have a gun. Being a gang member today is much more dangerous.

But there is an even more important difference. Today, there is also a new type of gang, the drug posse. Like the gang that tried to recruit Johnny Boston, drug posses make money from buying and selling illegal drugs like heroin and cocaine. The principal source of income for today's gangs is street drug sales. This drug activity often requires gang members to rob or act as strong-arm men to protect drug dealers from takeovers. Large sums of money can be involved.

The drug posse may include boys as young as 12 or 13. The posse is controlled by drug dealers who are usually men in their twenties or thirties. These drug dealers work for a worldwide business that is controlled by businessmen and criminals, often from other countries. The money the gang member makes is a tiny fraction of the billions of dollars made by selling illegal drugs.

At one time, gang members challenged authority because it was considered part of the way that boys became men. Or because the members wanted to show they had heart. But today's gang killings have less to do with ideas about manhood or heart. Instead, they are usually about drugs and money.

Chapter 5

Why Do Young People Join Gangs?

In *West Side Story*, the gang members sing a song called "Gee, Officer Krupke." In the song, the gang members make fun of different ideas about why young people join gangs:

> *Judge: The trouble is he's crazy.*
> *Psychiatrist: The trouble is he drinks.*
> *Social Worker: The trouble is he's lazy.*
> *Judge: The trouble is he stinks.*
> *Psychiatrist: The trouble is he's growing.*
> *Social Worker: The trouble is he's grown.*

Are gang members crazy? Do they join gangs because they are hooked on drugs? Do they come from broken homes? Are gang members simply no good? Is poverty the answer? Or is being part of a gang simply something that happens when kids grow up?

One of the most famous stories about a gang is the novel *Oliver Twist*, written by Charles Dickens.

Oliver Twist lived in England. When he was very young, he was sent to a foster home, where he was beaten and almost starved. He escaped to the city. There he joined a gang led by a crafty man named Fagin.

Sometimes the boys in Fagin's gang would pretend they were crippled and beg. Sometimes they would steal. At night, they had to give all the money to Fagin. If they kept anything back or tried to run away, Fagin would beat them.

When Oliver joined the gang, he knew little about how to survive on his own. The other boys taught him. They would call him a sissy if he tried to avoid doing dangerous or illegal things.

Fagin was like a father to Oliver. He made sure Oliver got food. He protected Oliver from the bigger boys. Oliver became a beggar and a thief. Like the other boys in this gang, he gave everything he had stolen to Fagin.

Why did Oliver join Fagin's gang? Here are some ideas to think about.

Poor Parenting

Oliver was placed in a foster home when he was very young. He believed his natural family didn't want him. And the people in the foster home beat and starved him. Could this be why some youngsters join gangs?

Gangs can seem appealing to teens who feel outcast and in need of
a sense of belonging.

In the 1950s, some people came to believe that gangs were the result of poor parenting. They thought that children became rebels when their parents beat them or were too strict, not letting them have any control over their own lives. They also thought children might join gangs when parents didn't seem to care about them or gave them everything they wanted. These children became bored and broke the law just for kicks or to get attention. This explained why some kids in the suburbs joined gangs.

Later, people came to believe that gangs were the result of the growing number of *broken families*. A broken family is one with only one parent (usually the mother) in the home.

Children need to feel loved and accepted by their parents. When parents do not respect their children, physically abuse or ignore them, the children may look for love, respect, and attention elsewhere. One place they can turn to for the respect they don't get at home is a gang.

A boy who feels like a nobody in his family or at school may feel really important with his friends when he gets money from selling drugs or stealing. This activity gives him a "rep" (reputation).

Children need parents who care enough about them to say no and set limits. They also need to learn standards to help them tell right from wrong. Children can get these rules and standards from either their mother or father, or from both parents.

Peer Pressure

Oliver Twist was encouraged to do things that were wrong by the other young people in Fagin's gang. This is called *peer pressure*. Peer pressure is another reason young people may join gangs.

Every young person needs to fit in with a group of friends. You probably dress as your friends do, wear your hair the same way, and listen to the same kind of music.

A *peer* is someone who is like you in a number of ways. You and the people your age that you spend time with are called your *peer group*.

Peer pressure can make you do things you would not do on your own. Part of growing up is taking risks. But peers may push you to do things that can cause you to hurt yourself or others. Or they may pressure you to do things your parents, teachers, and other adults have told you are wrong. Oliver Twist believed stealing was wrong. But when the other boys put pressure on him to break the law, Oliver went along. That is peer pressure.

Many young people join gangs or break the law because of peer pressure. Peer pressure can make anyone feel confused about what is right. It is often hard to stand up to your friends.

Young people may think, "If I don't do what they're doing, my friends won't like me." We all want to be liked. Because of this, it may be hard to ask yourself, "If these are my friends, why are they trying to get me into trouble?" It's hard to say no.

Poverty

Another common reason for joining gangs is *poverty.* People who live in poverty are poor. Often, they can only afford to buy the most basic things they need for survival.

Oliver Twist was poor. Instead of buying expensive things, he had to steal simply to survive.

Everyone sees expensive cars, stereos, and designer clothes on television. But many families cannot afford to buy these things for their children. This is not the families' fault. They may simply be poor. Or, like Johnny Boston, their parents may not make enough money to buy expensive things. Some families have different values. Rather than spend money on expensive clothes or cars, they believe in saving money for more important things.

In some poor neighborhoods, gang members are the only people who have any real money. Some young people get angry because they can't have the things others have. Their anger may lead them to find other ways to get these things. It may lead them to join a gang or break the law.

But many young people have legal jobs. If you have a job, the work you do may not be as exciting as some of the things that happen in gangs. But you can feel good about the money you make. You don't have to hide what you do from your family. You don't risk going to jail. And you are not in danger of being shot because of what you do.

Chapter 6

Breaking the Law

When young people break the law, they often do it as part of a gang. Young people who are arrested for breaking the law are called *delinquents*. Here is a list of the ten most common offenses young people commit:

- Truancy (failing to attend school)
- Incorrigibility (refusing to obey parents or teachers)
- Immoral or indecent conduct
- Using drugs or alcohol
- Running away from home
- Associating with thieves or with violent or immoral persons
- Constantly using vulgar language
- Violence
- Being in a place where illegal activity is going on
- Holding an illegal job, like selling drugs

Gang-Related Offenses

Gang members are well known in school. When something goes wrong, the gang member is the first to be blamed. Gang members have to protect their "reps." This often means doing things that make it hard to stay in school, and impossible to do well if they do stay in. So gang members usually stay away from school and become truants.

Being in a gang almost always means disobeying your parents. If the gang comes first, trouble builds at home. Gang members stay out late at night and don't respect curfews. Or they have weapons or drugs in the house, endangering themselves and other family members. Gang members who can't be controlled by their parents are called *incorrigible* and can be arrested.

A natural part of growing up is wanting independence from your family. Almost all kids sometimes think that being free of parents and family responsibilities would be great. But, joining a gang may mean no more school, no more church, no more sports, no more respect from your family. These are all the things you need to really grow up.

Some parents have to call the police or use violence to control their children when they have become involved with gangs. This often leads gang members to run away from home. Many of these young people become homeless or live in shelters.

Joining a gang also makes it easier to get hooked on alcohol or drugs.

Many gangs break the law. As a member of a gang, each person shares responsibility for the actions of the group.

Status Offenses

Most acts for which juveniles are punished would not be crimes if committed by adults. Acts that fall into this category are called *status offenses*. This means they are only crimes because the person who is committing them is below a certain age, usually 18.

Persons who are arrested for status offenses are brought to *juvenile court*. There, they are treated differently from adults. In juvenile court, the young person talks directly to a judge. The judge listens carefully and tries to do what is best for the child.

Delinquents can also be sent to special jails, sometimes called *reformatories*. These are often large facilities that are strict but not as tough as prisons. Because more and more juveniles are committing serious crimes like murder, many people believe they should be treated like adults and sent to adult prisons.

Some Facts about Delinquents

• Most youngsters commit acts that could be judged delinquent.

When children are asked about the offenses in the list, almost all admit that they have broken the law at least once in their lives.

• Kids from any background can be delinquent. That includes middle-class suburban kids or inner-city kids no matter if they are white, African American, Hispanic, or Asian American.

Society has many *prejudices* about who breaks the law and who should be in jail. A prejudice is a hostile attitude toward certain people or groups that is not based on the truth.

Gang members are arrested for breaking the law much more often than persons who don't belong to gangs. That may seem unfair. But it is a fact, and it means you are at greater risk of being arrested if you join a gang.

- All in all, only a tiny percentage of those who commit delinquent acts are picked up or brought before a court.

Does that mean it is worth joining a gang and breaking the law? Remember that joining a gang means giving up a lot that may be important—things like school, family, friends, church, sports. And, most important, it can mean giving up your independence or even your life.

- Although gang violence is rising, the overwhelming majority of violent crimes (at least 80 percent) are committed by persons over the age of 21.

Although thousands of young people join gangs, the vast majority of kids do not. Most young people—like most adults—respect the law. They also respect their parents as well as their pals. Most kids find ways to take risks and seek adventure that don't involve guns or violence. These young people prefer to be positive role models for younger children.

Gangs are not just for boys. Many girl gangs exist in today's inner cities.

Chapter 7

Girls, Gangs, and Sex Roles

Some people think gangs are only for boys. There *are* many more boys than girls in gangs. But girl gangs have been around for a long time,too. And they still exist.

Some Facts about Girl Gangs

There have been changes in girls' roles since the 1950s. Some people believed that as girls became more independent, their criminal behavior would be more like that of boys. They thought girls would fight and steal. They also thought girls would be more involved in gang violence. But this view turned out to be wrong. The ratio of boys to girls in street gangs has stayed where it has always been—at about ten to one.

A female gang is usually tied to a male gang, and the two gangs' names are often similar. For example, one famous male gang was called the Amboy Dukes. Their sister gang was called the Amboy Queens. Girl gangs have their own leader, or "Godmother." Often the members choose boyfriends from their brother gang. But they are forbidden to become romantically involved with boys from a rival gang.

The decision to join a girl gang usually depends on the girl's willingness to "get down," or fight. Gang wars between rival girl gangs are common. But fists and knives are usually used, not guns.

The girl gangs may organize shoplifting rings, *panhandle* (ask passers-by in the streets for money), and hide their brother gang members' weapons and drugs when the police are around. Boys often stop being gang members after they've been badly hurt or gone to prison. But girls often remain in gangs until they've had their first child.

Sex Role Expectations

Sex roles come into play in gang violence in a number of ways. Sex roles refer to the expectations we hold about how boys and girls should behave. Much of the fighting among boys starts because of these beliefs.

Many boys believe that girls are their property. A boy might believe that his girlfriend should do whatever he tells her to do. When another boy spends time with his girlfriend, the boy might think he has to fight to show who is boss.

After school, Donna and Bob walked down the street to get a hamburger. They were sitting at a table discussing an upcoming football game. Donna was excited about the band that was playing after the game.

Rich, Donna's boyfriend, walked in and saw them. He didn't know Bob. Suddenly Rich was very angry. "Who does she think she is?" he thought. He walked over and said loudly to Donna, "Who is this guy? What are you doing here?"

Donna looked embarrassed. "Please don't be so jealous," she said. "Bob's a friend from school."

Rich said, "You're lying to me. You're a tramp. You've been sneaking around behind my back." He continued to call her names.

Bob said, "Hey, leave her alone. She's telling you the truth."

Rich grabbed Bob. "Shut up, or you've had it."

If Rich and Bob belonged to gangs, what do you think would happen next?

Some people have trouble communicating their feelings, and this can also cause fights. Many boys are brought up to think that males should not let others know when their feelings are hurt. So they use anger to cover up their feelings of hurt. They would rather fight—even if they are afraid and know they may be hurt physically—than admit they can be hurt emotionally.

Linda and Mike had been going out for several months. When they went to a friend's party, they were sitting on the couch listening to music. Paul walked over to say hi and then began joking with Linda about school. When Paul left, Mike was furious and tried to make Linda leave the party. Linda refused and Mike grabbed her arm and pulled her up. When Paul came over to ask what was wrong, a fight started. Because Paul and Mike were members of different gangs, the result was a rumble.

In the first story, Rich was jealous because he believed it made him small for his girlfriend to talk to another boy. He really had no right to question Donna, tell her whom she could talk to, or call her names. How else could he have handled the situation? How could he have told Donna what he was feeling without starting a fight?

In the second story, Mike could not express that he felt uptight when Linda didn't pay attention to him. He could not simply say, "You hurt my feelings." Instead, he felt he had to hurt both Linda and Paul physically.

Remember that old-fashioned sex role expectations can cause serious problems. For example, no boy has a right to treat a girl as if she were his property. Also, knowing that it's okay to talk about your feelings can give you another option when you think you have to fight.

Chapter 8

The Guardian Angels

They are mostly male, and mostly black and Hispanic. They always travel in groups. They ride the subways and prowl the streets at night. They wear their colors and are constantly looking for trouble. A typical gang waiting to prey on innocent people? No. This gang's policy is to protect people. That is why they call themselves the Guardian Angels.

They are one of the most talked about gangs in the United States.

Curtis Sliwa and the Guardian Angels

Curtis Sliwa had the ability to lead. When he put his mind to something, he followed through. When Curtis was 15, he decided to start a clean-up campaign in Brooklyn. Soon he had five tons of trash in his front yard. The next year, he entered a burning house and helped to rescue seven people.

Soon Curtis Sliwa was known all over New York City. Then something happened that changed his life. A dress code was introduced in Curtis's school. When he joined the protest against the code, he was kicked out of school.

Before long, Curtis was named assistant manager at a McDonald's in the South Bronx. Curtis knew karate, and part of his job involved keeping peace in the restaurant. Soon he had organized a group of sixty-three students as a "Rock Brigade" to clean up the neighborhood.

Next he decided to take on crime. Why not organize a gang, he thought—an anti-crime gang.

First he decided the members should wear red berets. Then he decided on white T-shirts because the kids who joined his "gang" would not have money for fancy jackets.

The Growth of Curtis's "Gang"

At first Curtis was only able to find 12 others to join his group. They decided to call themselves The Magnificent Thirteen. To join the group, you had to be in school or have a job. Soon the "gang" had grown to 48 members, including Chinese American, Hispanic, African American, and white young people.

The members began to ride on the "muggers express," a subway line in New York with more

Curtis Sliwa (left) started his gang, the Guardian Angels, as a way to help protect cities against crime.

robberies than on any other line. And they began
stopping crime. Things got safer simply because
the Guardian Angels were there. By 1980, the
group had grown to more than 700 members, including many women.

Pretty soon, people in other cities wanted the
Guardians in their communities. Curtis could no
longer run the Guardians by himself. He needed a
second-in-command. The person he found was Lisa
Evers. Lisa was from Chicago. She also knew
karate and was as courageous as Curtis. In 1981,
she became the national director of the Guardian
Angels. Her first job was to set up a Guardian
group in Atlanta. Soon there were gangs of Guardian Angels patrolling unsafe neighborhoods in
almost every major city in the United States.

Guardian Angels must be models for their community. You cannot join the Guardians if you have a
criminal record. When you join, you must go
through a three-month training period. Members
are frisked to make sure no one is carrying drugs
or weapons.

By 1983, there were over 3,000 Guardian Angels.
Today there are more than 5,000.

Chapter 9

Another Way of Fighting

For as long as we can remember, young people have joined gangs. Society has tried to stop youth gangs in many ways. For example, laws have been passed against running away. Laws were also passed against many of the things young people often did in gangs, like drinking beer and skipping school. Children who were homeless were sent to live with families in the country. People hoped that when a child who had lived on a city street moved to a farm, he or she would stop making trouble.

Society also tried to stop gangs by forcing children to go to school until age 16. In the 1950s, many people hoped to eliminate gangs by giving youngsters more opportunities to participate in sports and other activities.

But none of these approaches seems to stop young people from joining gangs. As long as the causes—things like peer pressure, poverty, and abuse—exist, kids will continue to join gangs.

New problems are posed by today's gangs, the violent gang and the drug posse. To deal with these, we need another way of fighting.

Stopping Youth Gangs

One way to stop drug gangs is to organize with your neighbors.

*In Detroit, one of Clementine Barfield's children was killed by a member of a gang. When another of her children was shot and almost died, Clementine decided to do something. She called other mothers and fathers who had lost sons or daughters to violence. They decided to form a group to stop gang violence. They called their group SO SAD. The letters stand for "**S**ave **O**ur **S**ons **A**nd **D**aughters." When mothers and fathers in other cities heard what Clementine Barfield had done in Detroit, they started groups like SO SAD.*

Richard and Deborah Dozier live in New Haven, Connecticut. There is a rock house on their block. A rock house is a place where you can buy crack, a form of cocaine. The Doziers told several drug dealers to leave the area near their house. Shortly afterwards, police raided the rock house. The drug dealers blamed the Doziers. They threw a fire bomb at their house. Luckily, the Doziers were able to put out the fire before anyone was hurt. But the Doziers were very angry. Members of their church rallied to their support. Marches and meetings against drugs were held throughout the city.

A Neighborhood Watch is another way to fight gangs. There are not enough police to watch every street all the time. So neighbors have to watch out for each other. They take turns being the lookout. If they see something suspicious happening, they call the police. The police make special arrangements with neighborhood watch groups. They give them a special number to call and special stickers for their windows.

Another place to fight gangs is in school.

A man named Joe Clark became principal of East Side High in New Jersey. East Side High was considered one of the worst schools in the United States. When Clark arrived, there was graffiti on the walls and teachers were afraid. Gangs roamed the halls, beating students and openly selling drugs. Clark acted fast. He got twelve strong security guards. Then he expelled all the drug dealers and gang members. Then he put padlocks and chains on the school doors to keep the troublemakers out. He introduced a school dress code so students could not wear gang colors. Student grades improved, and teachers and students were no longer afraid. Recently a movie called Lean on Me *was made about Joe Clark and East Side High.*

When Joe Clark became principal of East Side High in New Jersey, he fought bravely to restore order and improve education there.

Another way to prevent violence is by learning nonviolent ways to settle conflicts.

Two years ago in Fulton County, Georgia, the Board of Education decided to combine six high schools into three. A lot of time was spent talking to the teachers and parents about what the change would be like. But no one talked with the students. So when school started, fights broke out between gangs from the different schools. Many kids were suspended from school. At athletic events, shots were fired. At one school, all dances were canceled for an entire year.

Luckily, not all the students wanted violence. A campaign called "Stop the Violence" was formed.

Leaders from each school met every two weeks at one of the schools to talk things over. At the first meeting everyone was afraid a fight would break out. Gangs from one school blamed gangs from the other schools for starting the violence. When the students couldn't agree, they asked a local talk show host to help them. Together, the students made a plan. They learned nonviolent ways to resolve conflicts. The high school students went on to train students in the middle schools to settle conflicts without violence.

Remember Johnny Boston? He had a difficult choice. KSI, the gang in his neighborhood, had many things he wanted—friends, money, excitement, loyalty, and a "rep." He was impressed by the gold chains and the new sneakers. At first, it seemed easier to say yes. So he took the money from the drug dealer.

After much thought, Johnny decided to talk things over with his mother. Johnny came to see that joining KSI would only mean big trouble. He would have problems at school—and he liked school. He would be able to meet girls—but only certain girls. He would have money—but if he was arrested, he would lose everything. Worst of all, he would have to lie to his mother, stop seeing his new friends, and be putting himself in danger.

Johnny Boston said no. Johnny learned that coping with gangs is not something you can do alone. It is not weak to ask for help. It can save a life.

Glossary—*Explaining New Words*

alliance A pact. When persons or groups decide to do something together.

emblem Sign or symbol. Something you wear to show that you belong to a particular group.

immigrants People who have recently moved from another country.

initiation What you have to do to become a member of a group or gang.

kingpin Leader, boss of a gang.

peer A friend or equal. Someone who is like you and whose opinion you care about.

posse A new type of violent gang, usually small, that makes money from selling drugs.

reputation What others think about you.

rumble A fight, usually between two gangs.

turf The place you defend. Your block or neighborhood.

wilding A gang rampage in an area, looking for trouble and—often—stealing, beating, and doing other serious crimes.

Where to Get Help

Local Resources
- School personnel: including teachers, counselors, social workers, psychologists, nurses, and principals.
- Police Officers
- Members of the Clergy
- Crisis Intervention Centers
- Shelters for Abused Families
- YWCAs
- YMCAs
- Department of Social Services
- Emergency 911

You can call these phone numbers from anywhere in the United States.

National Center for Missing and Exploited Children (exploited means used, and often abused, children): 1-800 843-5678.

Child Abuse Hotline: 1-800 222-8000

Runaway Hotline: 1-800 321-6946

Community Information and Referral Services (a United Way agency, available 24 hours) (601) 263-8856 or 1-800 352-3792.

Español Violence Hotline: 1-800 942-6908.

Linea Directa Para Adolescentes Desparaecitos: 1-800 222-3463.

Narcotics Anonymous Line: 1-800 522-5353.

For Further Reading

Barden, R. *Gangs.* Vero Beach: Rourke, 1991.

Berger, Gilda. *Violence and Drugs.* New York: Franklin Watts, 1989.

Landau, Elaine. *Teenage Violence.* Englewood Cliffs: Julian Messner, 1990.

Licata, Renora. *Everything You Need to Know about Anger.* Rosen Publishing Group, 1992. Good coping mechanisms for dealing with anger.

McShany, Rosen, eds. *Street Gangs, Gaining Turf, Losing Ground* New York: Rosen Publishing Group, 1991. Fiction and non-fiction from around the world on gangs in many different countries.

Rubin, Theodore. *The Angry Book.* New York: Ballantine Books, 1990. This book helps you deal with feelings that often lead to fights.

Stark, Evan. *Everything You Need to Know about Domestic Violence.* New York: Rosen Publishing Group, 1991. This book will help you deal with violence in the home.

Webb, Margot. *Coping with Street Gangs.* New York: Rosen Publishing Group, 1990. This book explains why children join street gangs and what can be done about it.

Index

Alcohol, 25, 33

"Bloods," 14
breaking the law, 41–45
broken families, 38

Capone, Al, 31
cocaine, 14
colors, 11, 15
"Crips," 14

Deliquents, 41
    facts about, 44
Dickens, Charles, 36
drive-by killings, 19
drugs
    and gangs, 14
    dealing, 7, 11, 12, 14, 26–27,
        34
    taking, 25, 33, 42

Ethnic groups, 33
Evers, Lisa, 54

Foster homes, 36

Gang-related offenses, 42
gangs
    and guns, 6, 11–12, 26
    business of, 34
    ethnics in, 13
    girls in, 6, 47–50
    history of, 29–34
    initiation, 18–19
    joining, 19
    language and rituals of, 29
    learning about, 13–20
    loyalty in, 16
    members of, 6, 13
    organization of, 13, 14
    in prisons, 14
    questions about, 7, 21–27
    quitting, 25
    reasons for joining, 35–40
    risks of joining, 20
    sex roles in, 47–50
    social, 25
    in the US, 6
    violent, 14–15
graffiti, 14–15
Guardian Angels, the, 7, 51–54
    growth of, 52
guns, 11–12, 26

Homelessness, 42
Juvenile court, 44

Kingpin, 16, 27

Marijuana, 14, 25, 33
mobs, 31

Oliver Twist, 36, 40

Pager, 9, 12
panhandling, 48
peaky blinder, 29
peer groups, 39
peer pressure, 39
prejudices, 45
poor parenting, 36
posses, drug, 7, 14, 16, 34
poverty, 40

prejudices, 45
Prohibition, 31

Reformatories, 44
rough music, 29
runaways (from home), 42

Sliwa, Curtis, 51–54
status offenses, 44

Tattoos, removing, 7
turf (gang's territory), 13, 20

Values, 40

"Walking the line," 16, 25
Watkins, Brian, 19
West Side Story, 33, 25
"wilding," 20

About the Author

Evan Stark is a well-known sociologist, educator, and therapist as well as a popular lecturer on women's and children's health issues. Dr. Stark was the Henry Rutgers Fellow at Rutgers University, and associate at the Institution for Social and Policy Studies at Yale University, and a Fulbright Fellow at the University of Essex. He is the author of many publications in the field of family relations and is the father of four children.

Acknowledgements and Photo Credits

Cover photo by Chuck Peterson.
Photographs on pages 2, 8, 43, 53, 58, Wide World Photos; pages 15, 18, 23, 37, Chris Volpe; pages 17, 24, 46, Stuart Rabinowitz; page 28, Gamma-Liaison; page 31, © Bayarel Didier/Gamma-Liaison; page 32, © W. Miles/Gamma-Liaison.

Design/Production: Blackbirch Graphics, Inc.